A Human for Huxley

This book is dedicated to my husband, Bruce, my daughter, Olivia, my first editor, and my son, Noah, for his constant encouragement.

This book is also dedicated to the thousands of women and men who work in the animal shelters, helping those animals find their own special humans.

ENGLISH TO
DOG DICTIONARY
AR ROOF..........EXCUSE ME.
ARF-ARF..........PARDON ME.
OW-WOW-WOW-WOW..........I'M OVER HERE.
RUFF RUFF..........THANK YOU.
WOOF..........YES.

This is heavier than it looks, Huxley thought.

I just can't do it!

This is hopeless!

Huxley was sad. He wanted to play fetch, but it was too difficult to throw and catch the stick by himself. He needed help.

"Go get it boy!" said the human walking by.

"Ruff! Ruff!" Huxley said.

Huxley was hungry.

I need to get this bag open, Huxley thought.

Plunk. Plunk. Plunk. Huxley's food fell on the floor.

Huxley wanted to eat food from a bowl just like his friends, but it was too difficult to pour by himself. He needed help.

"Here you go sweetheart," the nice human said. *"Ruff! Ruff!"* Huxley said.

Huxley's belly felt itchy.

"GRRRRRR!" Huxley growled.

I just can't reach! Huxley thought.

Huxley needed a good scratch, but his short arms could not reach his belly. He needed help.

"Help has arrived," the young human said
as he scratched Huxley's belly.

Huxley looked around at all his friends in the park who had no trouble playing fetch, getting fed, or their bellies scratched. He felt a little sad.

Huxley had an idea. He was going to find his own human to adopt. He knew a place with a lot of humans.

"Arf-arf!" Huxley said to the human with the pizza. There was no reply.

"Ar roof!" Huxley said to the human trying on shoes. There was no reaction.

"Ow-wow-wow-wow," Huxley barked at the teenaged humans. They didn't even notice him.

Huxley was discouraged.

Huxley had to think of another place to look

for his own human.

"Arf-Arf!" Huxley said to the librarian.

"Quiet," the librarian said.

"Ar Roof!" Huxley said to the human reading in the comfy chair. "Shhhh!" the human responded.

"Ow-wow-wow-wow!" Huxley said to the human typing on the computer. "Shush!" the human said.

Huxley was even more discouraged.

Huxley thought and thought. He now knew the perfect place to look for his human.

"Arf-Arf," Huxley barked at the running human. The human kept on running.

"Ar roof!" Huxley barked at the human with the tennis racket. The human kept on playing.

"Ow-Wow-Wow-Wow!" Huxley barked at the young human. It was the nice young human who scratched his belly earlier.

"Hi boy! Would you like to come home with me?" the young human asked Huxley.

"WOOF! WOOF! WOOF!" Huxley answered.

www.ingramcontent.com/pod-product-compliance
Lightning Source LLC
Chambersburg PA
CBHW040303100426
42811CB00011B/1351